NEW AMERICAN
BEST FRIEND

NEW AMERICAN
BEST FRIEND

Poems by
OLIVIA GATWOOD

—

Published by Button Poetry / Exploding Pinecone Press
Minneapolis, MN 55403 | http://www.buttonpoetry.com

—

Cover Design: Nikki Clark

ISBN 978-1-943735-10-5

CONTENTS

The constant project of our girl selves, seeming to require odd and precise attentions.

—Emma Cline, *The Girls*

JORDAN CONVINCED ME THAT PADS ARE DISGUSTING

They make your panties smell
like dirty bike chains.

We were sitting on her mother's plastic-coated floral couch,
one of us in a swimsuit, the other sworn to layers.

The water was her selling point and I was terrified of tampons
      or rather
terrified of the undiscovered crater, the muscle that holds and pulls
      and keeps and sheds.

She said, *I'll do it for you*
and yes, we had seen each other naked many times,
we had showered together and compared nipples, wished to trade
the smalls and bigs of our respective bodies.

So it wasn't unnatural, really, when I squatted on the toilet seat
and she lay down on the floor
like a mechanic investigating the underbelly of a car.

With plastic syringe in hand, she wedged the packed cotton into me;
this was what I saw last
before blacking out and collapsing onto the tile—

Jordan, Blood Scholar, in a turquoise bikini
saying, *Now you are ready to swim.*

ODE TO ELISE IN EIGHTH GRADE HEALTH CLASS

She wasn't wrong
when she accused me
of staring. I was.

A profound observation,
What are you, gay for me?
As if my body
could be flipped
solely in the wake of her,
some kind of reverse
conversion therapy

which wasn't wrong either,
I had never pined
so badly for denim
to slip down her lower back
upon taking a seat

to reveal the fuzz
along her spine,
that which she likely
wished to remove,
begged her mother
for hot wax
like we all did and
how I hoped
she never would

prayed that no boy
would call her *beast*

my secret joy, Elise,
who melted the tip
of her eyeliner pencil
and let it sizzle
in her tight line

Elise, who gathered
six of her friends
and threatened
to jump me in the alley

Elise, who taught me to bury
a lighter in my fist,
so that if I ever took my shot
at least I wouldn't break my hand
on her pretty, pretty face.

THE FIRST SHAVE

I am nine.
We are bored
and Karen is dying.

We drove to Austin
that summer
so Sarah's dad—

who described Karen as
the great and impossible love
of his life, who taught us

the word *lymphoma* and then,
the concept of the prefix,
how it explains where the tumor lives—

could say goodbye.

The house is a rind
spooned out by the onset of death,
what's left is a medicine cabinet

full of razors & we are hungry
& alone & sitting
on the living room floor

where the light
from a naked window
slices the hardwood

like melon, brandishes
each, individual fuzz
on my scabbed calf

a field of erect, yellow poppies
& we have been alive as girls
long enough to know

to scowl at this reveal
& what better time
than now to practice removal.

Once, I watched my mother
skin a potato in six
perfect strokes

I remember this
as Sarah teaches me
to prop up my leg
on the side of the tub

and runs the blade
along my thigh, *See?*
she says, *Isn't that so much better?*

Before we left Albuquerque
her father warned us,
She will have no hair

a trait
we have just
begun to admire

except, of course
for the hair he is talking about
that which we hold against our necks,

that which will get us
husbands or compliments
or scouted in a mall,

eventually cut off
by our envious sisters
while we sleep.

BUBBLEGUM OR BRUISE

blush so pink it can't be powder
blush so pink and icing whipped
blush so pink i saw it on a commercial
blush so pink on cable television
blush so pink the model dips her finger in the jar
and slides it across her cupcake cheeks
so pink i save up seven dollars
so pink i walk to the pharmacy
so pink the makeup aisle is a soda fountain
strawberry milk in the mini carton
blush so pink like panther
like raspberry lemonade feather boa baby shower
so pink like holiday for love
blush so pink i wish it was my name
blush so pink i take it to the paint store
this color, i say, paint the whole house!
blush so pink i wear it to school
blush so pink daddy says,
those are some pink cheeks
blush so pink the whole seventh grade stares
so pink they call me clown
so pink but not my color
blush so pink my best friend
covers her palm with her sleeve
wipes it across my face,
now her sleeve is fairy road kill
sleeve so pink like bimbo shame
sleeve so pink she can't get it out in the wash
sleeve so pink for the rest of the year
blush so pink it never leaves the house again
except for on that sleeve,
blush so pink like milkshake bloodstain
blush so pink but only in private
blush so pink like lesson learned
blush so pink like *learn*
what your face is good for
everyone is nauseous

blush so pink like rash, infection
so pink like itch and burn
blush so pink like *learn*
how to love quieter, circus girl
it's making us all sick.

LIKE US

and we grew up and hardly mentioned
who the first kiss really was—a girl like us,
still sticky with moisturizer we'd shared in the bathroom.
- Marie Howe, *Practicing*

I had perfected the story before telling it—
rehearsed it during imagined interviews
in the shower—it was 2004 and his name
was Noah, my best friend since grade
school, we wanted the first kiss to be a safe bet,
the kind we could feel good about telling
our kids but didn't end in heartbreak or sex.
I liked this small pill of a story,
how it made my life bite-sized
and interesting but still, there
was always Margot
how her spit was tacky and
harsh from gummy new growth
how I was the boy because I liked
my sneakers and got my hair cut
at the barbershop, how we
confessed to each other the places
we had rubbed our crotches against:
arms of recliners, spoons, the seams
of denim and now, each other's
thighs, sometimes in our swimsuits,
jumped in the river just so we'd have
an excuse to wear them, an excuse
to shower together, change together,
linger when the other one peeled
the one piece down their damp torso
and how we both felt bad about
the game so we did it on the pull-out
bed, that way, when we were finished
slamming our tiny, moth bodies
against the porch lights of each other,
we could tuck the cot away and

the bedroom would go back to
the way it was before—
Curly-Sue, nail polish, pastel coiled
phone cord, strawberry milkshake
designed by her mother to ensure she would
grow up the kind of girl who cries
when the boy does not love her—
in an instant.

LIBERTY

When the blonde counselor showed up at Christian camp,
the boys stopped being fun.

She arrived, a stack of bubblegum
suitcases next to her—

one reserved only for her headbands—
and the boys stopped mid-dribble,

one foot in the river,
macaroni necklaces slid off their strings and onto the floor.

Rumor was, the camp dog only had three legs
because a boy swung his gun during rifle practice

just to drink a glimpse.

We should be team building not breaking,
she said one evening, after canceling Capture the Flag.

All of the boys said *Hallelujah*, suggested trust falls.
All of the boys held out their hands.

I declared war when she banned potato chips.
She called for vegetables, the cooks planted a garden.

I swore I would find her guilty for something—cigarettes
in her tennis shoes, an expired condom between book pages.

I waited for her to pull last night's meal
from her throat with the hook of two fingers,

for two pairs of feet in the shower.
But each time I hid in the bathroom stalls and spied,

she only flat ironed her hair in thick, lemonade chunks.
Each time I pretended to sleep, she only whispered to God

at the foot of her bed, as creased as a pleated skirt.
Each time I followed her to the yard, she only raised the flag,

watched it float up into the sunrise,
a quiet hum of *America The Beautiful* under her breath.

She did not know that when the boys
lined up in four, straight rows to sing the anthem,

they were singing it for her. When they praised
the land of purple mountains, of shining seas,

when they belted *O' Beautiful,* it was for her.
When they sang *America, America,*

they were calling her name.

LESSONS ON REAPING WHAT YOU SEW

We wasted whole days on the 66 bus
cruising Lomas for thirty-five cents
just to remind ourselves, and whoever else
decided to look, that we were capable of transience.
But mostly, it was for the air conditioning.

Jordan wore long sleeves that summer
and told the seventh-grade counselor
that she had *fallen into a bucket of knives*
which, I remember thinking, was not untrue,
based on the use of the verb *fall* in other phrases,
to imply it was not particularly accidental
but more so situational, like how one might
fall in love or *fall in with a group of bad girls.*

The bus wagged and groaned from my house
to the park in about thirty minutes, and then
there was the small twitch in my belly
when we saw the circle of shaggy-headed boys
beneath the overpass, a pile of bikes and skateboards
next to them like metal bonfire, or the cloud of sweet,
grape smoke that met us before they noticed we had arrived.

Jordan was good at bartering for her presence; as soon
as she spoke you would forget what it was like to live
without her. Before the boys could decide to do something
that didn't include us, she would make light of exactly
what it was we had that they didn't, usually in the form
of a complaint like, "I just want to take off my bra already,
can you help me?" And because I was *with her,* a title
I would have preferred over my own name,
they would assume me next in line to be stripped
as though whatever pain Jordan felt, I felt too.

It wasn't long before we were in the center
of the circle playing with each other's hair
while they watched, flaunting the way we could share

our bodies where they weren't allowed. It was a gift—
to know a boy's desire and catch it in a jar, to watch it bash
its body against the glass, salt on a spooned-out snail.

If I could freeze the moment here, I would—
head on Jordan's thigh, emptying a peach
Primetime into my throat. But of course the
debt billowed toward us with its jaw unhinged
and we were asked to walk how we speak,
to release whatever we had emptied into the
boys, name the city we had built in their bodies.

Jordan knew I was a nervous girl. Maybe that's why
she kept me around, I made her look wise,
a broken wristwatch on the forearm of her life.
And I remember when she saw me tremble,
held my cheek, smiled weakly, said
I've got this, as though she knew all along
she would have to tame the circus by herself.

I stayed lookout while she took the oldest one
behind the bushes and did whatever she did best,
which, from what I understood, was the ability
to take and take and take.

Jordan's choke becomes a groan becomes
a laugh and I breathe for the first time.
She emerges from the tall grass, water welled
in her bottom lid and smiling, like a teary-eyed mother
at a dance recital. He says something about *talent, stamina,
ahead of her time* and she calls him a liar and he grabs her ass
with a newfound sense of purpose and walks us to the bus stop
with a draped arm over the back of her neck while I float
a few feet away and when he climbs on his bike to leave
Jordan yanks him by the shirt and demands two cigarettes.

One for now to get out the taste
and one for later when I remember what I did.

By now, the sky has cracked into a shrill, blue—
a final shriek before the sun plummets behind the Sandias.
It is July, just past evening rush hour and the city is a dying flame,
the gap of silence between hissing cars growing longer and longer
and longer with each, tender minute.

You yourself are unsure
whether to remain frozen in time
or to grow upward with the coming rain.

—Danielle Boodoo-Fortuné, *Joshua on the Edge of Thirteen*

PORT OF SPAIN, 2002

I couldn't bury my face into the sheets at the Sunset Motel
to scream because they smelled like wet mold.

Daddy sold the house in America & we rented an apartment
next door to Mr. Biswas & it had one bed & we had four people

but it also had cable & instead of cicadas
there were car alarms & my brother

freestyled over the steady scream
& we couldn't close the windows

because I was allergic to the air conditioner &
we all cursed my name for that but we all sweat

for me, we all got bit & in the morning Daddy had me hold
his waist as we crammed into the yellow maxi

& the driver saw my uniform & said
You must be smart 'cause you can't be rich

& at first there was ketchup & then
there was shado beni under the stairs

& I learned to make chow and pholourie
& a girl with a birthmark in the shape of Tobago

lent me her bike & the boys' league said I could play
& I always got extra dumplings in my cup of corn soup

& I finally learned the metric system
& I got taller & my period

& when I stood at one end of the Savannah
I couldn't see where it stopped

& America became a city
where I never owned a camera

& had no proof that I had ever lived there
except for a few scars

they kept calling this place an island
they kept saying we were floating

& small

THE ONLY THING I BROUGHT FROM AMERICA

are four scabs
and a ten-dollar gift card
for international phone calls.

My father walks me to school every day,
until he finally buys a 1989 Nissan station wagon
with damp seats and an apple cinnamon
scented tree that flutters under the rearview mirror.

Reina is upset that I am American
and not rich. These two details disrupt everything
Reina has ever been made to believe in the church
of MTV, in which she learned
that along with a new American best friend,
Reina deserves a new American
best friend's mom—suburban queen—
and a new American best friend's brother
who will take her to second base in our basement,
but unfortunately for Reina,
we don't have a basement, we live in the Sunset Motel
where I collect snails and eat chicken and ketchup
sandwiches for dinner.

Girls don't play sports, the boy says
to Reina as he crumples up
his sandwich tin-foil into a firm,
silver ball. *Except for Olivia.*
But Olivia is American.
Reina whips her neck to glare
at me, I am guarding the wicket,
ready to bruise whatever the boy throws
before she can whisper *dyke* into the wind.
But still, she slips it into my ear and prances back
to the shifty-eyed, hairless girls in the corner
of the yard, their ring fingers dawned in the
jeweled promise of their kept bodies.

When Reina tells the teacher that I am staring
at her in the locker room,
I walk to Long Circular Mall and buy a gold,
plastic rosary from the quarter machine
(all of the rich girls wear rosaries)
pull my hair back into a taut bun and
polish my calves with my mother's lotion.

Reina says I can sit with her at lunch
as long as I never play cricket again.
I tell her it was just a phase, in the way
that the motel was a phase, the car and the smell
and the hair on my body—all a phase—
but the thing about pretending to be rich,
is you can sculpt the language of money,
lie about the helicopter, the vacations, your maid—
the way you call her only by her first name—
but I know, no matter how many times I speak
of Mary, my imaginary helper, I can't spit her out
like I would if she were a real woman,
who dressed me every morning, like Reina,
who scowls while she eats hand-rolled dolmas
and I haven't played cricket in three weeks,
instead, I take a bite of my mayonnaise sandwich
and complain about Mary's cooking
while the blacktop shines
and the boys sweat
at the other end of the yard.

Reina says I am lucky
they let me play, because the pitcher
is the cutest guy in school, so she asks
if I will teach her
the game and I tell her
I don't really know the rules,
Americans don't play cricket, I say,
I just know to hit and run,
and I know this is the right answer
because she repeats it under her breath,

Americans don't play cricket,
Americans don't play cricket,
I don't play cricket
because my best friend is American,
better than you, better than your stupid game.

DRY SEASON, 2003

The bush fire off Long Circular Road
has finally found its temper
and is barely a whimper—
an orange hiccup in the night—

our parents are no longer certain
that the blaze will swoop us kids
up by the ankles but, as we all know,
the dry season does not release its grip

just because the burn became civilized.
The mountain is raw and transparent,
the trees dissolved into black milk
and what happens behind the thick

of the rainforest is not a game of Jumanji
anymore—the howler monkeys have gone
silent, the flock of green parrots too,
and the pack of dogs, who usually live

amongst them, now wander our yards,
tongues flapping, ribs loud against
their skin. It is Christmas, but I,
and my American imagination,

wouldn't know that based
on the fevered sky, the thirsty
animals seduced to mainland,
our desperation for something wet.

Shauna and I jump on a water pipe
until it cracks in half and a stream
as thick as a can of Coke
shoots so high we think,

for a moment, it might never come
back down, but it does, in heavy fists

on the tops of our heads and soon
we are twice our usual weight in water.

What a strange sight, two soaked girls
wandering a parched city. When the neighbor
asks where we found the rain, we do not tell
him we released it from the city's

veins ourselves, that the drought forced us
to build a counterfeit sky and in its final
hours, the sun swells and bursts
and we are nearly dry when we notice

that ash is fluttering down
like gray snowflakes
and we do as any child would—
we catch them in our mouths

until our palms
and tongues
and teeth
are black.

That summer I did not go crazy
but I wore
            very close
very close
            to the bone.

—Dorothy Allison, *To The Bone*

BACKPEDAL

the boys and i are playing quarters with double shots of vodka and i am winning. by winning i mean i am not one of the boys but i am the next best thing. by the next best thing i mean i am a girl and i am drunk. every time i miss a shot, johnny gets to flick a quarter against my knuckles and now my knuckles are bleeding onto my thighs but every time i make a shot i get to knock back a throat full of liquor. i slam down the glass until it cracks up the side and now the game is about who will still drink from it, who will risk shards in the belly, who will cut up their insides for a pack of newports and it's not that i even want the cigarettes, it's just that i am not afraid of blood which is also part of being a girl. but being the only girl means making yourself lose when you've won too much so i bounce the coin off the rim of the shot glass and let johnny slice me open. in thirty minutes, johnny is dragging me out of the bathroom by my wrists and i can hear him saying something about blood on the carpet, about a drunk girl in the house who is staining everything and i think that means i must be the champion of quarters. johnny is the kind of guy who sleeps with a gun, not women. but johnny is always the one inviting me over for a game of quarters and sometimes i wonder if this is how johnny fucks. like maybe he is the kind of man who only screams when he is underwater or lets me feel how strong his fingers are without actually touching me. maybe that's why we're all here, even the boys, to let johnny hold us like a barred window. i work a double one day a week and on this day, don't answer johnny's call. by one day a week i mean two men break in and shoot johnny in the temple for two thousand pills and i am scraping pasta from a businessman's plate into the trash. at some point i'll tell you why i didn't go to the wake. i guess i never really knew johnny like that. by that i mean sober or in a church. when i say i didn't go to the wake i mean i drove by his house every day for two years and the for sale sign never got taken down like the house would always be johnny's, like maybe the whole town knew what happened there. like maybe no one could get rid of the blood.

THE AUTOCROSS

The men at the autocross say I could be useful
in a garage because I have tiny hands. I can reach
the deepest corners of an engine like a house maid,
make it all brand new.

They say I'm different than other girls,
the ones splayed out across the hood
like a brand new paint job. The ones who like the taste
of old oil under a fingernail, how easy it is
to zip off a navy jumpsuit.

The men at the autocross don't believe I know
the difference between a four cylinder and a V6 engine
but they keep me around anyway because
I don't take up much space. They aren't bad guys.
They don't know my name, never asked,
just call me Girl Driver, which is what I am.
The men aren't wrong.

When I clock in a tenth of a second faster than Mike
in the '98 Miata, the men say it's because I don't weigh shit.
They don't know my name but they call me cheater.

The men re-tighten my bolts *just for safe measure.*
The men open my car door, *Ladies first.*
The men are always helping.

One man asks how I reach the pedals.
One man asks where my daddy is.
One man opens his trunk and says,
Bet you're small enough to fit.

FOURTH WEEK OF TWO-A-DAYS IN JULY

Us girls with all of our stuff—
our cleats and shin guards
and Ace bandages and headbands
to keep our bangs back

our sports bras and spandex
and everything else
that preserves the body, the bones,
our most promising tool

our expensive sneakers—
I got mine at a place called
Play It Again Sports,
where rich kids sell
their one-season-used Nike cleats

with the side laces that claim
a purpose they don't actually fulfill,
got long sleeves to wipe the sunscreen
that bleeds into our eyes—

got a fifteen-second water break
ten minutes ago and now
we've got six miles around the golf course
that is supposed to be the color of money

but around here, looks like horse food.
Lauren passes me on the second loop,
spits, and the wind sprays it in my face
like some party bitch blowing mean confetti

and now my view is her blonde ponytail
whipping like a breakneck pendulum.
Lauren, who says I smell like piss
on a good day, is the only one who broke off

the rest of us are a cloud of bats
circling the dead
grass. It is three o'clock,
eight years into the drought

and when Jackie stops to vomit
in the ditch, I hang back
while she hacks up nothing.
Next to us, nestled in the dirt

is a syringe and a rubber tie-off
a spoon bent in the shape of a daffodil
black tar burnt to the mouthpiece,
scattered like an abandoned highway shrine.

I swat her on the back,
remind her of the college scholarship,
the scouts and the ironed jerseys,
all that money waiting for her feet.

THE SUMMER OF 2008 AT ALTURA PARK

after Hanif Willis-Abdurraqib

The boys took me to the corner of the park
that was most hidden by trees to tell me the news.
Are you going to kill me, I joked and they
each pulled a handful of grass from the ground
and shoved it into their mouths.

I waited in silence while they looked at me
the same way my father did
when I choked on a piece of bread at dinner,

What happened was, Jordan said
While you were away, Eric continued
It wasn't that big of a deal, JoJo choked out
like a skipped rock across the river of his throat

and there they sang like a choir of boys
whose voices have not yet plummeted
to the bottom of a well

Your boyfriend left the party with a girl
and this time, this time he came back
covered in blood, his shirt was soaked,
he threw it away, drank whiskey for the rest of the night
half-naked, when we asked what happened
he said she got a bloody nose
said she got her period, said she was a virgin,
said she liked the pain, said sometimes you can fuck
a girl so hard you break something
no other man could reach.

I waited for them to finish
like I often did then with men, to stop speaking
of this girl who I imagined
must have been blonde.

And when they sealed the confession,
I wove my fingers together in my lap
like a patient wife, knitting her own body,
pushed the girl back down to the bottom of the river
said, *What do you mean, "This time."*

He merely hoped, in darkness, to smell rain; and
though he saw how still
I sat to hold the rain untouched
inside me, he never asked
if I would stay.

—Rita Dove, *Wiederkehr*

MANIC PIXIE DREAM GIRL SAYS

Have you heard this record? Manic Pixie Dream Girl says,
Let me save you with this record.

Let me put the headphones on for you
and smile while you listen. Cut to your point of view

watch me smile as you listen. Hear that?
That's the sound of you becoming a better person.

I'm gonna paint a picture of a bird on your beige wall
without your permission and you're gonna love it.

And you thought you hated birds.
See me, encouraging you to take risks?

Manic Pixie Dream Girl wants you to do something
you've never done before like smile, or go swing dancing.

You wanna know my name?
You never call me by it anyway.

If I had to guess, it would probably be a season
or after a dead actress who you loved as a child.

But this isn't about me, this is about you
and your cubicle job, your white bedroom

your white Honda, your white mother.
Manic Pixie Dream Girl says, *I'm going to save you*

says, *Don't worry, you are still the lead role.*
This is your love story, about the way I teach you to live.

Everything they know about me
they will learn when it is projected onto you.

Watch the way you pick up my bad habits
and make them look good.

Manic Pixie Dream Girl talks too much
says bad words out loud and cries at the commercials.

That makes me a funny woman, right?
The kind people like to laugh at?

It's easy to root for you when I act like this—
so disagreeable, such a manic dream.

Dream Girl, your almost broken accessory.
Manic Pixie Dream Girl says

Let's play make believe with my body.

I'll be a vintage dress with an empty prescription
bottle, good girl, just bad enough

a burp
and a curtsy,

let me be not too pretty
hair fried from all of that pink dye

sex when you need it puppet when you're bored,
let me build myself smaller than you,

let me apologize when I get caught acting bigger than you.
Let me always wait for this, let me work for this.

The convenient thing about being a magical woman
is that I can be gone as quickly as I came

and when you are a whole person
for the first time, the movie is over

Manic Pixie Dream Girl doesn't go on,
there's no need for her anymore

Manic Pixie Dream Girl is too dream girl
and you just woke up.

Once, I told you I was afraid
of my father and for a moment, I looked so human

the audience lost interest
you saw the crow's feet at the sides of my eyes

and a small chip on my front tooth.
I looked just like everyone else.

THE ANTHEM I HAVE SUNG

our heads let go
of their dead parts

weave into our lovers'
carpets long after we have left

our mothers send us to buy draino
after we break the pipes,

hair dressers turn off the sink, mid-shampoo
to throw away a handful of our dark mess,

twisted knots stick to our legs and backs
wet rats laid on the edge of the tub—

the joke between women that this
is how we mark our territory like glitter

or breadcrumbs, his bedroom a trunk
carved with nothing but my name—

rip a day's worth from the brush, unclog yourself
and praise the way you are always growing back.

this anthem i have sung of my own shedding mane
until i stood ankle deep in the bath

and pulled her scraps
from his choking drain.

ODE TO THE WEDDING DRESSES IN GOODWILL

after Ada Limón

I like the ugly ones best
with lace collars and satin
ballooning shoulders
pointy breast cups and itchy
hoop skirts, two dozen buttons
up the back, all to be sealed
and then undone individually
chastity belt of the spine;
I like how, unlike the collapsed
La-Z-Boys and mugs with chipped lips
they have presumably only been used
once, sometimes there will be remnants
of a nervous bride, Saturn's Phoebe ring
sweat stain around the neck, which speaks
nothing of the size, but rather
the near invisibility until closer inspection
as sometimes they are hung up high
in the window for passersby to point
and say, *The only thing more tragic*
than selling a wedding dress to a
second-hand store is buying
a wedding dress from a second-hand store,
but really, if I'm being honest,
I like the riddance of the ritual,
the furious picture of a woman
shoving the corpse of the corset
into a garbage bag, dropping off
the heap of tulle in the back alley
like black market icing, and perhaps
one day—after the furniture has been rationed,
the ring sold, bought back her name
—she will return to visit the dress,
and it will be there on the racks,
gaggling with the other gowns,
crammed side by side like front row
fan girls, living.

WHAT SEX BECOMES

I remember being a waitress
on Valentine's Day and loving
the newness on a couple's face,

how I watched, like the only patron
at a matinee, as they shared
everything they ate.

I would deliver their sundae
with an extra cherry—
the one she would slide into her mouth—
a preview of what was to come.

I felt like a school teacher
who goes home to no children,
a cab driver without a car,

a therapist who cries
in the middle of the night
and can't figure out why.

THE RITUAL

you agree to do it if he lets you lie on your side.

      you tell him it hurts less this way.

you tell him you will close your eyes.

      you tell him it feels nice. like spooning.

you place your hand on the wall in front of you. when he pushes,

    your hand against the wall acts as a cushion for your face.

you have grown accustomed to discovering all of the ways

    you can make the pain intangible. unrecognizable.

for instance, preventing a nosebleed.

    and so, you are between him and your hand, against the wall

window-shopping for the next room, the front door,

    outside, where it is lunchtime and your father is repairing something

on the car you ruined. the boy goes fast and apologizes.

    you do not tell him everything you've learned.

that this, your body, a small knot, and his, in combat, is what you know.

    he pulls your hair back from your face

says *thank you, i needed that. i'm hungry, let's eat.*

THE SCHOLAR

the house is heavy with sour burning fish / when i leave / my clothes will smell / of seared salmon / sulking men on the train / will tidy their backs / twist their necks / in my direction / assume my thighs used bait / you know the thing we learn in grade school / about cheap girls' bodies / how they carry the sea / i make the train smell like gowanus / trash river lady / all for you / you are back home writing a book / on the kitchen floor / told me this morning / you met someone else / she lives in europe / but you have more in common / like religion / your names / sound nice together / i ask for my things / you give me a garbage bag / i ask for my coat / you beg me to leave it / *it smells like you* / you say / the last time we made love / you asked me / if i was scared / i think you wanted me / to say yes / when we go to bed / all of the women scale the fire escape / perch on the rust / cackle and sing / *you can tell how much he loves her* / *by how he sleeps* / *not at all* / *not at all* / not at all

ODE TO THE WORD PUSSY

I could devote my time to justifying
your name by defending the feline.
But what about the lioness,
I might say, *colossal queen*
of the animal kingdom, or even
a house cat, twitching mouse caught
in its claws, how could my body not be that?

But this debate doesn't interest me,
or you, I would imagine.
For years I have been a bystander
to your wasteful adoption,
a slingshot against men who can't take
a blow to the stomach and I've left
in search of a less tiresome way
to praise you. An ode to you will be
for your sound, your good word, for each
small leap across your rippling body

for instance, how clever you are to make
the human press their lips together
before spilling out your name,
to gather the air between the flesh
and push it out in a flaccid alto hum,
let it hang there for moment
like a foreign thread, the audience not sure
if it's fishing line or spider web,
they wonder if it will be *pulse* or *pulverize,*
they pray for pure and then, the vowel
is snatched back, tongue pressed
against the arch of the mouth,
sibilance suspended in whir, a fly in a jar
this is the climax, everyone has already winced
and covered their prudish ears, so
the muscle falls like a whale slapping the ocean
with its back, the lips open
to a smile and out comes the happy soprano

of an elongated *e*, and what better place
to end than here? To conclude this forbidden
moniker than with the pitch of joy?

Speaking of joy, let's indulge in your sermon
for a moment—Webster defines you as inflated
or swelled, which is to say you should always be just that,
fat with blood and want even in the quiet
of the work day, in transit or under the dinner table,
I will always imagine that this is your synonym,
not coward in the dugout, not frail or timid,
not the name on the sign stuck to a small boy's back

and yes, many will call you profanity, diminish you
to a whisper, but this is an ode to your double s,
that unmerciful hiss, and the way it screams
in quiet gossip like a dog whistle, punching
through the veil of night.

ODE TO MY PERIOD UNDERWEAR

I didn't purchase you as such,
you grew into the role,
earned your name
after the first stain
and admittedly
now I am careless
with your fabric
no fear of the overflow
as I trust you will not
mind another scar
and yes, once you were
brand new
bought in the name
of some boy who I wished
to see me unmarked
and clean as his mother's
kitchen counter
perhaps once you were
even called
the good pair
which is not to say
you are the opposite now
but that you gave
new meaning to the phrase
in the way that a good car
is often one with six digits
in the odometer
isn't that the greatest evolution,
for something to be good
and then to become more good
in its thorough use
you, keeper of a thousand
not-pregnant surprise parties
instigator of the exhale
proof that no matter
how many years
I have spent here

I will never
get the hang of this
and even though
I have shoved you
to the back of the drawer,
strategically folded
so that your forever mess
was not revealed,
I have also reveled
in the fossil of you
yes you, relic
of age thirteen
and also
twenty-three
hoarder of the blot,
we all have at least
one of you to slide up
our winter legs
wiggle in your loose grip
and this too is a kind
of ceremony, the choosing
of you, I mean
and the washing, too
the folding and wearing
and washing again
and at last the ruin
the ritual of the spill
your national anthem,
your ever-changing flag.

ALTERNATE UNIVERSE IN WHICH I AM UNFAZED BY THE MEN WHO DO NOT LOVE ME

when the businessman shoulder checks me in the airport, i do not apologize. instead, i write him an elegy on the back of a receipt and tuck it in his hand as i pass through the first class cabin. like a bee, he will die after stinging me. i am twenty-four and have never cried. once, a boy told me he doesn't "believe in labels" so i embroidered the word *chauvinist* on the back of his favorite coat. a boy said he liked my hair the other way so i shaved my head instead of my pussy. while the boy isn't calling back, i learn carpentry, build a desk, write a book at the desk. i taught myself to cum from counting ceiling tiles. the boy says he prefers blondes and i steam clean his clothes with bleach. the boy says i am not marriage material and i put gravel in his pepper grinder. the boy says period sex is disgusting and i slaughter a goat in his living room. the boy does not ask if he can choke me, so i pretend to die while he's doing it. my mother says this is not the meaning of unfazed. when the boy says i curse too much to be pretty and i tattoo "cunt" on my inner lip, my mother calls this "being very fazed." but left over from the other universe are hours and hours of waiting for him to kiss me and here, they are just hours. here, they are a bike ride across long island in june. here, they are a novel read in one sitting. here, they are arguments about god or a full night's sleep. here, i hand an hour to the woman crying outside of the bar. i leave one on my best friend's front porch, send my mother two in the mail. i do not slice his tires. i do not burn the photos. i do not write the letter. i do not beg. i do not ask for forgiveness. i do not hold my breath while he finishes. the man tells me he does not love me, and he does not love me. the man tells me who he is, and i listen. i have so much beautiful time.

ODE TO MY BITCH FACE

you pink armor, lipstick rebel
steel cheeked, slit mouth
head to the ground, mean girl.

you headphones in but no music
you house key turned blade
you quick step between streetlights
strainer of pricks and chest-beaters,
laughter is a foreign language
to your dry-ice tongue.

resting bitch face, they call you
but there is nothing restful about you, no,
lips like a flatlined heartbeat
panic at the sight of you,
scream for their mothers, throat full
of bees, head spun three-sixty
exorcist bitch just trying to buy a soda
just trying to do the laundry
just trying to dance at the party
then someone asks you to smile
and the blood begins to riot
smile, and you chisel away at your own jaw
smile, and you unleash the swarm
into the mouth of a man
who wants to swallow you whole.

one theory is that you were born like this
but i don't believe it. you came out screaming
and alive and look at you now, look at how
you've learned to hide your teeth.

what's wrong with your face, bitch
your face, bitch, what's wrong with it?

bitch face, i don't blame you for taking
the iron pipe from their hands and branding yourself
with it, for making a flag out of your body bag.

another theory is that you put it on every morning
screw it tight like a jar of jelly
but i don't believe that either.
you woke up like this and have been for years,
how can you sleep pretty
when there are four locks on the door
and the fire escape feels like break-in bait?

they will tell you home is safe zone
no, bitch face is safe zone,
bitch face is home
bitch face is cutting off the ladder
willing to burn in the apartment
if it means he can't get in.

ODE TO THE WOMEN ON LONG ISLAND

after Jennifer Givhan

I want to write a poem for the women on Long Island
who smoke cigarettes in their SUVs with the windows
rolled up before walking into yoga, who hack and curse
in downward dog and Debra from the next block over, who
has strong opinions about Christmas lights after
New Years, who says that her body isn't what it used to be
but neither is the economy or the bagels at Rickman's Deli
so who really cares, who, during Shavasana, brings up
the rabbi's daughter, who got an abortion last spring,
and Candy in the corner, who is mousy and kind but
makes a show of removing her diamond ring before
class because *it's just too heavy,* calls Debra hateful
and the class takes a sharp inhale through the nose
then out through the mouth. and after class, after Candy
rushes home to check the lasagna, Debra lights up
a smoke and calls her best friend Tammy

> *So then the girl calls me hateful*
> *hateful, can you believe it? What a word*
> *some kind of dictionary bitch over here*
> *and so you know what I says? I says*
> *you don't know the first thing about hateful,*
> *wanna know what's hateful? Menopause.*

And it doesn't really matter if Debra actually said that
to Candy (which she didn't) because Tammy is so
caught up that Candy called Debra hateful (which she did)
that next week when Tammy runs into Candy while
shopping in Rockville Center and Candy asks Tammy
how she's doing, Tammy will adjust the purse strap
on her shoulder and say, *We all have a little coal*
in our stocking, Candy, and Candy will shuffle away,
certain that Tammy knows something about her marriage
that she shouldn't and she doesn't, she just loves
Debra, who just has a lot of opinions and had Candy given
her the chance to finish her sentence, Debra would have
talked about the reproductive rights march she went to

49

in the sixties and the counterproductive sex-shaming
methods of organized religion. I want to write a poem
for the women on Long Island, whose words stretch
and curl like bubblegum around the forefinger, who
ask if I have a boyfriend and before I answer, say

> *Don't do it. Don't ever do it. You know*
> *my friend Linda, she's a lesbian,*
> *like a real lesbian and whenever I go*
> *over there, she lives on Corona over by*
> *Merrick, by the laundromat you know where*
> *I'm talking about? Whenever I go over there*
> *and see her and her wife, what's her name*
> *I can never remember the girl's name*
> *anyway whenever I go there I says you know*
> *what I need? I says, a girlfriend, that's what I need.*

The women on Long Island smoke weed once a month
on the side of the house after their husbands —Richard Larry
Gary Mike or Tony —go to bed, they let their teenage
daughters throw parties in the basement while they watch
the Home Network upstairs and keep a bat by the couch
in case anyone gets mickied, even if it's their own son
who did the drugging, the women on Long Island won't
put it past any man to be guilty, even their kin who,
after all, have their husband's hands and blood and
last week, when a girl was murdered while jogging
in Queens, the women on Long Island were un-startled
and furious, they did not call to warn daughters.
They called their sons. Took their car keys, their coats,
locked the door and sat them at the kitchen table,

> *If you ever, and I mean ever, so much as*
> *make a woman feel uncomfortable*
> *I will take you to the deli and put your*
> *hand in the meat slicer, you think I won't?*
> *You hear me? I will make a hero out of you.*
> *With mayonnaise and tomatoes and dill and onions*

I want to write a poem for the women on Long Island
who, when I show them the knife I carry in my purse,
tell me it's not big enough, who are waitresses

and realtors and massage therapists and social workers
and housewives and nannies and tell me they wish
they would have been artists but

    Life comes fast. One minute you're taking typing classes
    for your new secretary job in the World Trade Center
    and the next it's all almost over, life I mean, but I kicked
    and screamed my way through it, and so will you,
    I can tell by the way you walk. One more thing
    when they call you a bitch, say thank you.
    say thank you, very much.

Acknowledgements

—

Thank you to the editors of the following journals, which first published the following poems:

"Jordan Convinced Me That Pads Are Disgusting" and "Backpedal" *Muzzle Magazine*

"Bubblegum or Bruise," "Liberty," and "The Only Thing I Brought From America" (formerly titled "When the Prettiest Girl in School Asks You to Play Cricket at Recess") *Winter Tangerine*

I would like to thank the kids I grew up with in Albuquerque and Port of Spain for their resilience, support, and exceptional bravery. Without you all of these stories would be nonexistent. Stephanie on Aliso Street, Taylor C., Taylor H., Avry, Noah, Alec, Meg, Joanna, Marissa, Monique, Carolina, Annie, Gabby, Leigh, Amelia, and Jenny, thank you for surviving with me. Thank you, Shauna and Stephanie in Flagstaff for choosing me as your friend.

Thank you to the people who worked patiently with me on this project since its very early stages and who have supported me in any capacity throughout this journey: Melissa Lozada-Oliva, Hieu Minh Nguyen, Giddy Perez, Mason Granger, Carrie Fountain, Megan Falley, Lissa Piercy, and Hanif Willis-Abdurraqib.

I am so grateful to everyone at Button Poetry for giving my work a place to live.

Lastly, to my family for giving me the freedom to be, despite the terror that sometimes resulted in allowing me to exist wholly as myself.

About the Author

—

Photo by Ashley Rose Hamilton

Olivia Gatwood is a nationally touring poet, performer and educator from Albuquerque, New Mexico. Her work has been featured on HBO and Verses & Flow, as well as in Muzzle Magazine, Winter Tangerine, HelloFlo and The Huffington Post, among others. She has been a finalist at the National Poetry Slam, Women of the World Poetry Slam, and Brave New Voices and currently performs at schools across the country as an advocate for Title IX Compliant education. She is a graduate of Pratt Institute's Fiction Program.

Other Books by Button Poetry

———

If you enjoyed this book, please consider checking out some of our others, below. Readers like you allow us to keep broadcasting and publishing. Thank you!

Aziza Barnes, *me Aunt Jemima and the nailgun.*

J. Scott Brownlee, *Highway or Belief*

Nate Marshall, *Blood Percussion*

Sam Sax, *A Guide to Undressing Your Monsters*

Mahogany L. Browne, *smudge*

Neil Hilborn, *Our Numbered Days*

Sierra DeMulder, *We Slept Here*

Danez Smith, *black movie*

Cameron Awkward-Rich, *Transit*

Jacqui Germain, *When the Ghosts Come Ashore*

Hanif Willis-Abdurraqib, *The Crown Ain't Worth Much*

Aaron Coleman, *St. Trigger*

Available at buttonpoetry.com/shop and more!